REESE'S Peanut Butter Cups

The Untold Story

REESE'S Peanut Butter Cups

The Untold Story

✦

Andrew Richard Reese

iUniverse, Inc.
New York Bloomington

REESE'S Peanut Butter Cups: The Untold Story

iUniverse books may be ordered through booksellers or by contacting:

iUniverse
1663 Liberty Drive
Bloomington, IN 47403
www.iuniverse.com
1-800-Authors (1-800-288-4677)

ISBN: 978-0-595-48707-3 (pbk)
ISBN: 978-0-595-60804-1 (ebk)
ISBN: 978-0-595-49107-0 (cloth)

Printed in the United States of America

iUniverse Rev. 10/17/08

This book is dedicated in loving memory of the Author's father, youngest child of H. B. and Mommy Reese.

Charles Richard Reese
1928-2005

Charles Richard Reese
1963

Contents

Foreword

I am so proud of this book, which documents the life of my father and brings back to me such fond memories of him. Andy has put a lot of work into writing this biography. I know he researched the family history for many years, and he found many things that I had forgotten about. Thanks to his efforts, his book's readers can learn about how hard it was for my father to make it in the candy business, and that he truly was a great man and a great father to us kids. I also appreciate the fact that Andy recognizes my mother's contributions in all of this. They say behind every good man is a good woman. She was a saint in our eyes, and all of us—my fifteen siblings and I—had a lot to be thankful for. The memories of Poppy and Mommy Reese, and my brothers and sisters, are now documented for everyone to enjoy.

Rose Amos (Reese) Rippon
Daughter of H. B. Reese

Preface

I cannot begin to tell you how many people over the years have asked me if I am related to the famous candy company that carries the family name. I typically inform them that yes, my grandfather was Harry Burnett Reese, better known as H. B. Reese, founder of the H. B. Reese Candy Company; but I also inform them that my father, Charles Richard Reese, was the youngest of sixteen children and that he had a twin brother named William. I do this because my family history is connected to the H. B. Reese Candy Company—to understand one is to know about the other.

My father was born on the eleventh of February, in 1928. This was an important year in our family's history, but it was also significant in the history of the business because 1928 was also the year my grandfather invented the famous REESE'S Peanut Butter Cups.

Advertisement distributed around 1933

Since childhood, I have heard many stories about how the candy company came to be. In 1973 I wrote my first version of the H. B. Reese family history. I was only thirteen years old at the time, but my little book included some old family pictures. My teacher, Mrs. Johnson, originally gave me a B but scratched it out and awarded me an A- for my childishly written masterpiece.

Thanks to my mother, I still have the school report, which sits next to me as I write this text. I find Mrs. Johnson's comments intriguing. We never know when a thoughtful, caring teacher is going to influence a young student. On the first page, Mrs. Johnson wrote, "A most informative letter, Andy!" I can only image what she really thought, and I wonder if she believed a word I wrote. I doubt she ever thought I would become a published author someday. (I had more than thirty-five errors in the report.)

As I grew up, though, I saw many published stories about my family. A little Reese family historical tidbit would appear in a newspaper where they quoted various first-generation family members. The candy company's own internal news pamphlet, called the *REESETTE*, covered our major family reunions. And occasionally a reference book on entrepreneurs briefly mentioned my grandfather's name and his contribution to the candy industry.

Then, in the summer of 1990, my aunt Rose Amos (Reese) Rippon decided to put together an eight-page report on our history to hand out at the next family reunion. She interviewed her oldest sibling, Mary Elizabeth (Reese) Pearson, and used their combined memories to create a short historical document. Everyone in the family wanted a copy, but over the years since then they have disappeared or faded from view, possibly stored in keepsake boxes in family members' closets.

In 1996, I created an Internet Web page that added to the historical content that Aunt Rose provided. Other family members continued to offer more and more information, including photographs. My second cousin, Brian Lauzon, created an informative video called *The Overflowing Cup* for, I believe, a college project. My brother Bradley Overholt Reese added his touch with a Reese family historical time line that he posted on his personal Web page.

Rose Amos (Reese) Rippon and (Author) Andrew Richard Reese

Here is a picture of me with my aunt Rose at our 1976 Reese family reunion. She has been an inspiration to me, not only because she created the eight-page document outlining the history of H. B. Reese that helped get me started on this book, but also because of a two-page outline of the Hyson family history, which would also help this project.

Aunt Rose's personal encouragement has been fundamental. Before I moved back to Hershey, she would insist that I stay at her house when visiting the area and share reminiscences with her. My father and Rose were quite close, since she was the youngest girl and he the youngest boy in their family. She has frequently visited our family in Florida.

◆ ◆ ◆

I was born February 2, 1960, in Hershey, Pennsylvania. My father and mother had a nice little house in the subdivision of Glenn Acres. However, my initial stay in Hershey was a short one. Father and Mother moved away from the area after the Reese family sold the candy business to the Hershey Chocolate Corporation in 1963.

Forty years later I moved back to Hershey with my wife, Elizabeth. Our adult children, Christopher and Valerie, followed us, and they both have their own homes nearby now.

I always wanted to live in Hershey. As a small child, I heard wonderful stories about our family legacy, which had begun there. It was only natural that Hershey held a special place in my heart. Whenever I traveled to Hershey for family reunions before I relocated there again myself, I felt a sense of peace come over me, as if I were finally home.

Despite my family background, or maybe because they don't know it, people ask me why I would want to move to Hershey. A currently popular phrase provides part of the answer: "Because I can." I am lucky enough to have a profession (information security consulting) that requires me to travel across North America, so it does not matter where I live just as long as it is reasonably accessible to transportation opportunities. In my case, the new Harrisburg airport is only five minutes away, and so is the AMTRAK station in Middletown, Pennsylvania. We live a short distance from the Harrisburg East exit to the Pennsylvania Turnpike and other major highway feeders going in all directions. Now, not only am I able to live in the home town where my family legacy was established, but I also avoid the congestion of a big city. I can travel anywhere with minimal notice and delays.

There are still other reasons why I moved to the area. I have studied martial arts since I was about eight years old and had reached a point in my studies where I wanted to learn things that are not taught in ordinary martial arts schools. I had become more of a martial scientist, wanting to learn the hidden secrets that only a few will ever know and master. For that reason, I sought tutelage from Grandmaster George Dillman, who is considered one of the best martial arts instructors in the world. He operates out of Reading, Pennsylvania, which is about fifty-five miles from my house. Since moving to the area, I have attended every martial arts training camp he has held. I am one of his master-level sixth-degree black belts in Ryukyu-Kempo, better known as the Okinawan style of Karate.

The Reese Family
Elizabeth, Andrew, Christopher, and Valerie

We have been here a few years now, and the township of Hershey still holds a strong appeal for its Reese family members. Conversely, many people from the town have come up to me and told me how great the candy company was when our family still owned it; however, if we go to local tourist locations, we do not see anything about the history of H. B. Reese. At least, I have not found any books worth reading on the history of candy making available for sale at any of these locations because they really don't talk about my grandfather and other family members. The information presented is also not always historically accurate. The history books on Milton S. Hershey are very interesting to read, and you can find them at tourists traps around Hershey; however, I have many stories about Milton S. Hershey and my grandfather that are not in any of these publications. Now, some of them are included in this book.

Despite the lack of literary evidence about our family's role in candy making, I have to admit that I love all the memorabilia floating around Hershey that promotes Reese's candies. You can buy pillows, key chains, coin purses, pens, pencils, postcards, posters, stickers, kitchen utensils, Reese dolls and characters, flip-flops, belt buckles, golf balls, cups, model racing cars, racing caps, racing jackets, drinking glasses, candy boxes and tins, lunch boxes, clocks, coloring books, memo pads, footballs, baseball bats, baseballs, baseball caps, basketballs, basketball backboards, magnet posting boards, many kinds of magnets, scarves, stocking caps, all the clothing you could ever want, and much more.

If you have not been to Hershey, Pennsylvania, you need to get moving because you are missing a lot. Be sure to check out the local attractions; it will take two or more days to see them. There are plenty of places to stay, no matter what your budget is. Each local store carries different memorabilia, so it is a good idea to do a little shopping around in the area to find your valued treasures. I try to make my rounds twice a year to purchase special items.

When I shop here, I cannot resist the temptation to buy something for my extensive Reese collection. We store most of these items in our house, in what we call the Reese's Room—and, yes, the room smells like milk chocolate and peanut butter. This was designed with family visitors in mind, my father in particular. He saw the location as it was being built and knew we had a special place designed for him; but he died in 2005, before he had a chance to stay in the finished room. My wife and I dedicated the Reese's Room to my father and the Reese family.

The Reese's Room Closet

All kinds of historic memorabilia line the walls of the room, and the closet is bursting with clothing, jackets, sweaters, trays, backpacks, Reese's candy, and much more. When we turn on the closet light, a blaze of orange and yellow assaults our vision. The bed is made up with milk-chocolate-colored covers, pillows that look like a REESE'S Peanut Butter Cup package, special Reese's quilts, little Reese's teddy bears, and all different sizes of dolls that look like the REESE'S Peanut Butter Cup man. The dresser drawers are filled to the top with Reese's candy bars, and we even created a special Reese's Christmas tree. In addition to the diverse collection, we have several original, rare photographs of my grandfather and many other family members. Everyone who visits our house wants to stay in the Reese's Room.

Family Reunion, 1976

Back Row: *Charles Richard Reese, Harry Burnett Reese Jr., Ralph Collins Reese, Edward Irons Reese, John Manifold Reese, and Robert Hyson Reese*

Front Row: *Clara Louise (Reese) Lauzon, Mary Elizabeth (Reese) Pearson, Rose Amos (Reese) Rippon*

My cousin, Harry G. (Pat) Lauzon, was responsible for coordinating the Reese family reunions over the years—literally for decades. Handling family reunions is no easy task and requires a variety of skills, as well as extensive effort. Reunion notices need to go out to all the relatives, and once here they want plant tours and places to stay, and special games and events to play and attend. Other necessities include: barbeque grills, beverage coolers, bathroom facilities, garbage collection, picnic tables, and lots of chairs. Then we need to provide transportation, cut the grass, clean the pool, arrange for all kinds of food, and complete more details than most people would ever imagine until faced with the project.

Pat has been a real trooper and like a big brother to me. Since he used to work at the Reese factory in Hershey, he has given me his copies of the *REESETTE,* the factory newsletter. Like Aunt Rose, Pat also gave me inspiration to write this book and offered many ideas about how to find information on the family. I thoroughly appreciate having him live so close to me, so we can visit each other frequently.

Family Reunion, 2004
Christopher Richard Reese, Harry G. (Pat) Lauzon, and Andrew Richard Reese

Over the years, the list of family members has grown considerably. When we take into consideration the sixteen children my grandfather and grandmother had, it is not surprising to know that their family tree has expanded to 178, with over 155 of these family members still alive today.

Pat eventually turned the reins over to me to coordinate the Reese family reunions, and I have used my knowledge of technology to help track where everyone is living and to send out personalized communications to family members as needed. I created a special address book for the family, which includes a short history inside. I also made a 211-slide presentation about our family history, for family events. It is fun to see pictures of relatives over the years as they grow and change.

Reese Family Reunion, 2004 – Three Generations
Andrew Richard Reese, Charles Richard Reese, and Christopher Richard Reese

During one of our reunions, I asked family members to bring their pictures with them so I could scan them, transfer them to electronic form, and redistribute them to other family members. We swapped many stories and historical facts related to the photographs.

Several family members asked me to write a comprehensive history. It was at this point that I decided to compose a formal book dedicated to our grandfather and, for me personally, to my father and son as well.

This book takes all the historical information I have gathered thus far and all the family stories told and heard throughout the years at our family gatherings, and presents it in a documented, informative, educational, and historical manner. I hope the local tourist locations in Hershey, Pennsylvania, will sell this book in their stores along with other Reese memorabilia. I also hope that candy stores around the world will find this book to be a neat little novelty.

Finally, I hope that you, the reader, will find this historical information interesting and inspirational, because I believe everyone should know about the other famous entrepreneur, aside from the town's namesake, who lived in Hershey, Pennsylvania: Harry Burnett Reese.

I present this book to you for historical, educational, and enjoyable reading.

Acknowledgments

I thank my father, Charles Richard Reese, and Aunt Rose Rippon for giving me the inspiration to write this book. Their memories and many stories added perspective to the historical information.

Thanks to my cousin Harry G. (Pat) Lauzon for all the time and energy he spent coordinating the Reese family reunions every year; I have pictures of reunions he arranged dating back to 1974. Especially now, I can appreciate the love and work he has given this family. I also thank Pat for the videotapes he made while interviewing many of the first-generation family members who recounted their fond memories of days past.

I appreciate the many editorial additions over the years that my father and my brother Bradley have made to my Web site on the Reese family history.

Thanks to all of the relatives who brought their photo albums to the Reese reunions and allowed us to scan the photos. Each picture has a story to tell, and now their memories can be shared with many others.

I appreciate the time other family members have taken out of their own schedules to review the contents of this publication. All of their children will now have their legacy documented for many generations to come.

Most of all, I want to thank my wife, Elizabeth, for the many hours she spent reviewing and recommending edits to this material and for being my supporting partner all these years.

Childhood

Harry Burnett Reese

Harry Burnett Reese was born on May 24, 1879, at a country crossroad (Frosty Hill Road and Stewart Road) known as the Frosty Hill Farm, near Muddy Creek Forks, Pennsylvania. His father was Aquilla Asbury Reese Jr. (1845–1914) of Baltimore, Maryland, the son of the Reverend Aquilla Asbury Reese (1812–78) and Anna Burnett (1811–92). Harry Burnett's mother was Annie Belinda Manifold (1854–1935), daughter of John Frosty Manifold (1804–88) and Eleanor Manifold (1812–96).

Muddy Creek Forks was within a few miles of Frosty Hill Farm. Back then, the town consisted of a post office, a store, a mill, and a train station. Today it is not much bigger and looks pretty much the same as it did in the late nineteenth century.

The ancestors of Reverend Aquilla Asbury Reese immigrated to America in 1680 from Wales. They initially moved to northern Virginia and then to York County, Pennsylvania.

Information on the Internet indicates the Reese family name originated from the Rhys Clan of Wales (270–1800). The information seems to correlate with the names, places, and dates of Reverend Aquilla Asbury Reese's family lineage. The lineage goes back to Jacitus and his son Paternus of the Red Robe. The clan apparently included a regional Welsh prince or king, Tewdwr Mawr Rhys, "the Greatly Adored" (ca. 997–1093).

Many people get nicknames as they grow up. We don't know exactly when Harry got his, but we do know where the nickname came from. The family has always referred to Harry Burnett Reese by his first two initials, H. B. It was a recognizable nickname that came to fit him well somehow.

It is interesting to learn how people, places, and things get their full names. Frosty Hill Farm, for instance, the place where H. B. was born, is named after his mother's father, John Frosty Manifold, who owned the farmland. We can easily see that H. B. got his middle name from his grandmother, Anna Burnett.

H. B. grew up in a lovely little white house in the farming region of York County, Pennsylvania, located near the base of a steep slope on the west side of Frosty Hill. The farmhouse was built in 1735 and has always been owned by family members. The house sits on the edge of 130 acres of farmland. H. B. purchased the land for fifteen hundred dollars from his mother's sisters Elizabeth J. Manifold and Mary C. Manifold, and H. B.'s mother, Annie, on April 2, 1901, shortly before his first child was born. He ended up selling the farm to his relative William G. Stuart on December 12, 1912, for thirty-three hundred dollars. The home is still owned today by relatives, Dale and Margaret (Peg) [Stuart] Leiphart.

Frosty Hill Farm—Birthplace of H. B. Reese
This picture taken in July 2006

Just down the hill from the house is a bubbling creek, and the picturesque view of this creek from the covered porch is incredible. It runs north and south between two ridges. These large hills provide a barrier of protection against hostile weather. Over the years, many of H. B.'s relatives and descendents have returned to the old homestead to fish in this fresh water resource, some going back on a weekly basis for that activity and to socialize with family members. A fishing derby takes place there every year. During this special event, automobiles pack the fields, and families line the creek, enjoying the life that H. B. grew up having in his backyard.

Frosty Hill Farm—Birthplace of H. B. Reese
This picture taken in July 2006

The landscape around the house is impressive, populated with many large trees, some of which are twice as tall and wide as the house itself. They add protection and beauty to the location. In addition, numerous levels of flowerbeds line the steep hillside; and a large dinner bell, easily heard hundreds of yards away, sits near the front walkway to the home. A small but productive smokehouse, still in use today, sits on the side of the hill. Farther up the hill are the remnants of another small building, once used to store ice, which could maintain the ice throughout the hot summer months. An outhouse (toilet) originally served the residents, but it became obsolete with the arrival of modern plumbing.

The house has gone through many renovations over the years. The original walls are still fairly solid; however, the floors have been re-enforced with steel beams. They still have a few dips and angles to them that visitors notice, sometimes with amusement, as they walk around on them. Occasionally they hear a creak in the floor here or there, and they can feel some soft spots in the wood. But considering the age of the house, the sounds add a special feeling of history and warmth.

The main entry door opens into the dining room, which used to be the original kitchen area. As we enter the room, to our left, a steep, narrow, winding staircase—its steps well worn—leads up to three bedrooms, a dressing room, and a bathroom. The larger bedroom, at the top of the stairs, features a small fireplace.

To the right of the dining room was once a bedroom, where H. B. and five of his children were born; but this room has since been merged with the old living room.

A large kitchen now sits off to the left side of the main living room, past the doorway that leads to the staircase. A wide doorway to the new kitchen has replaced a solid wall. This was a major undertaking because the wall was limestone, about three to four feet thick. The kitchen is now fourteen feet by nineteen feet. Off the main living room, we can walk out onto a very large, covered porch that overlooks a beautiful, bubbling creek. This is a new porch, built on top of a garage that has been added to the house. Originally, there was a smaller wooden porch; but the view of the bubbling creek is still the same.

The basement is unique in that it has a room that used to be the main living room, where everyone liked to gather. This room contains the largest fireplace in the house. The fireplace has a swinging hook mechanism that used to hold cooking pots. Now, a large wood-burning stove stands in front of the old fireplace. The room has a door that connects to the garage and another large room that is a nice little workshop area. There is also a door that opens to a fairly large backyard, which slopes down to the creek.

One of the unique features originally built into this home is a stream of spring water that actually flows into another area located off the basement living room. A small wooden door connects the fresh spring water room and the basement living room. A few well-worn stone steps open into the spring room. The spring water comes out from the side of the steep hill and into the house. The channel of water is about two feet wide and ten feet long; it is wide enough to dip a bucket into the running water. The water is then channeled into a pipe that runs down to the creek. When people see the other end of the pipe down by the stream they initially think it is waste water, but that is not the case. Considering the time period when this home was built, the fresh spring water was probably a highly attractive feature. There is nothing like having fresh spring water available inside your home, rather than having to go outside to get it from the creek or a deep well during the middle of a cold winter.

An old school house sits down the road from the farm. The building is still standing today, but barely. We can see math equations written on the board—but they are very faded. Many generations of family members learned their ABCs in this school, including H. B. and his children. A wooden stove used to sit in the middle of the classroom. During cold winter days, the entire class would scoot their desks close to the stove to stay warm. Today, trees virtually engulf the school, and the barely visible exterior shows no signs of paint. The wood has rotted to the point that a good swift wind would surely knock it down.

A recent visit to the old Frosty Hill Farm, in April 2008, found the room partition where H. B. and five of his children were born still standing. It is very interesting to see this home, knowing the history of the family. You can still eat dinner on the large, covered porch, and look out at the beautiful creek below. Imagine what it must have felt like in the summers for H. B. to live there, before air-conditioning. The value of having large trees, plenty of shade, and a cool, bubbling creek near the home is quickly understood.

Frosty Hill Farm—Red Barn

H. B. spent many years of his life at the Frosty Hill Farm. While living there, he helped work the hilly land. A few other family members owned land near Frosty Hill, and the whole group worked together to farm their land. H. B.'s mother had a rather large family. Today, the Manifold family has well over ten thousand descendants. Eventually, H. B. would marry into another large family, which owned a lot of farms in the area. There were always plenty of family members to help with farming.

Across the street from the north side of the house had been an old barn that had burned down. H. B. built another barn to replace it. A few silos used to stand next to the barns, but they no longer stand. The bottom floor of H. B.'s barn housed about forty to fifty cows. The stalls are still set up for feeding and milking cows, but ducks have taken over the bottom half of the building.

The rest of the barn, above where the cows were housed, is accessed from the back of the building by a little hill incline and some doors that can be rolled to the sides. This part of the barn housed a large stash of hay to feed the animals. H. B. carved his initials in the wood above a window in the upper left part of the barn, but we can see it only if we climb a very tall ladder. This part of the barn also housed the old farm equipment, such as plows and harnesses for oxen that were used to work the fields. H. B. farmed the land, but he also milked cows because doing so was a quick way to get cash.

When it came to earning money, H. B. was creative. Not only did he farm and milk cows, but he also built a pond where he raised frogs. He sold these frogs to restaurants in the Baltimore area.

Annie Belinda Manifold, H. B.'s mother, had two sisters who also lived with them at the Frosty Hill Farm: Elizabeth Turner and Mary Collins Manifold. It turned out that Annie Belinda and Mary Collins lived with H. B. for the rest of their lives.

H. B.'s oldest child, Mary Elizabeth, was born in the same house as her father. She spent her early childhood growing up on the farm and grew to love her aunt Elizabeth. When her aunt Elizabeth died in 1910, Mary Elizabeth was still a young girl; she remembered going into shock upon hearing the news of her aunt's death. Over the years, the two of them had developed a strong relationship.

H. B. Reese in Band Uniform, 1898

Farm work, making money, and family helped to define some parameters of H. B.'s childhood, but he had some fun, too. Music was one of H. B.'s passions, and he was an accomplished French horn player in the Muddy Creek Forks and High Rock Area Pleasant Grove Band of 1898. We have some original photos of him in his band uniform, taken at the Pine Grove Presbyterian Church in Sunnyburn, Pennsylvania. One photograph hangs in the hallway in front of the Reese's Room in the author's home in Hershey, Pennsylvania. There is also a newspaper clipping of him with the rest of his orchestra members: James McPherson, Samuel Jamison, Harry McCleary, John McPherson, Chester McCleary, William Dunlap, Robert McPherson, Robert McCleary, Morgan McDonald, James Wilson, John Shaub, Oscar McClure, John McCleary, William Bail, Charles Wilson, Calvin Randall, and Edgar Stewart.

Marriage

On August 1, 1900, H. B. married his love, Blanche Edna Hyson. Blanche was born August 20, 1882, near Gatchellville, Pennsylvania. Her mother was Mary Elizabeth (Markey) Hyson (1857–1952), and her father was Robert Bortner Hyson (1853–1930).

Blanche Edna (Hyson) Reese

H. B.'s mother-in-law, Mary Elizabeth, was very well dressed and a woman of admirable taste. Her hats were the best a person could buy, and she wore them elegantly. Linen napkins and tablecloths were always present at her dining room table. It is easy to see that she was a woman who inspired her husband, and was generally the type of person whom others emulate: graceful, elegant, refined, stylish, poised, charming, distinguished, and dignified. We can see her influence and taste in the way her family dressed and interacted with others.

Robert Bortner Hyson

H. B.'s father-in-law, Robert Bortner Hyson, was an educated man. He went to the public schools of East Hopewell Township and graduated from Stewartstown Collegiate Institute. In 1882, Robert was elected as the justice of the peace for Fawn Township, and he stayed in that office for twenty-four consecutive years. Robert was also the postmaster of Bridgeton, in York County, Pennsylvania, for ten years and a director of the Hartley Mutual Fire Insurance Company.

Eventually, Robert became a businessman and opened a big country store near his home in Bridgeton. He was a very prosperous merchant and the first person to own a car in the area. After a few years, he upgraded to a nice limousine, and Aunt Mary Elizabeth said H. B. occasionally served as Robert's chauffeur because his father-in-law lived only a few miles away. His store sold just about anything a person could need, including candy, cigarettes, groceries, dry goods, and clothing. Saturday nights were big occasions for farmers in the local area who would stop by the country store to buy and eat ice cream and peel freshly hung bananas. Robert also created a special room for Christmas gifts during the holiday season.

Robert's house was not far from the store; in fact, it was just behind the building, up on a hill. The house had a nice view of the store, Muddy Creek, and a train station that was located across the creek. By the year 1893, Robert had added a cannery to his operations, and by 1900, a creamery. He also operated a large cannery near Hopeside, Virginia, where his business canned large quantities of fresh vegetables, oysters, and fish. Managing a business in Virginia from Pennsylvania was a challenge since travel and communications were not easily accessible. Then again, Robert did live across the creek from a train station owned by the Maryland and Pennsylvania Railroad.

Eventually, H. B. moved to Hopeside to run the business's fishing operation. Truly, he had married into a well-to-do family, and he had much to give back. The support H. B. received from his father-in-law played a big part in his family's early survival. Several of Robert Hyson's brothers were also men of wealth.

My aunt Rose's two-page document about the history of the Hyson family reports that one of our relatives, Archibald Hyson, served in the Revolutionary War. He fought under General Washington at the Battle of Brandywine; more specifically, he served under Captain Alexander Ligget, Fifth Company. The evidence is that he was present when George Washington made his famous speech about being true to one's God, country, and home. This was personally relevant considering that Archibald Hyson came to America from Ireland before 1771. He settled in Hopewell Township, where he purchased a large tract of land from William Penn. The name Hyson was originally spelt "Eason," And at about this time, the last name was changed to "Hyson" because of the way it was pronounced.

Blanche's father was one of fourteen children, which was certainly large; but little did she or H. B. know how big their own family would become. Between 1901 and 1928, H. B. and Blanche's family grew to sixteen children, eight sons and eight daughters; hence, the parents' perennial nicknames, "Mommy" and "Poppy." H. B. was only called Poppy by those within the family; everyone else referred to him by his initials. However, everyone always called Blanche "Mommy Reese."

1928 Family Photo

Back Row: *Anna (Twohig), Ralph, Edward, John, Robert, Mary Elizabeth (Pearson).*

Front Row: *Rose (Rippon), Helen (Carson), H. B. holding Charles Richard, Louise (Lauzon), Frances (Hoke), Blanche holding William, Marjorie (Staggs), Harry B. Jr.*

Here is a list of their sixteen children, with dates and places of birth. Five of the children were born in the same home as their father (on the Frosty Hill Farm). H. B. was born in 1879, and his last child born at the farm, son Ralph Collins, came along in 1911.

	Children's Names	Date of Birth	Place of Birth
1	Mary Elizabeth	July 28, 1901	Frosty Hill Farm, PA
2	Robert Hyson	November 6, 1902	Frosty Hill Farm, PA
3	John Manifold	May 18, 1904	Ditchley, VA
4	Anna Alfreda	April 12, 1906	Ditchley, VA
5	Edward Irons	February 10, 1908	Frosty Hill Farm, PA
6	Marjorie Marie	February 4, 1910	Frosty Hill Farm, PA
7	Ralph Collins	November 24, 1911	Frosty Hill Farm, PA
8	Helen Grace	November 12, 1913	Woodbine, PA

	Children's Names	Date of Birth	Place of Birth
9	Clara Louise	September 6, 1915	Woodbine, PA
10	Frances Turner	April 1, 1918	Round Barn, Hershey, PA
11	Rose Amos	January 16, 1921	18 East Areba, Hershey, PA
12	Mildred Jane*	1923	18 East Areba, Hershey, PA
13	Harry Burnett Jr.	November 22, 1924	18 East Areba, Hershey, PA
14	Thomas*	1926	18 East Areba, Hershey, PA
15	William* (Twin Brother)	February 11, 1928	205 West Caracas, Hershey, PA
16	Charles Richard (Twin Brother)	February 11, 1928	205 West Caracas, Hershey, PA

**These three children did not survive to adulthood.*

Foundation

H. B. and Mommy Reese's first two children, Mary Elizabeth and Robert Hyson, were born at the Frosty Hill Farm. Considering that H. B. was born there as well, this home site served H. B. and his family for over a thirty-two-year period. The home was well protected from hostile weather, had a fresh water spring, was bought and paid for, and had been in the family for many years. It was near other relatives, was part of a farming and dairy community, and was not far from Baltimore, Maryland, or York, Lancaster, and Harrisburg, Pennsylvania. When we examine H. B.'s history, we see that Frosty Hill Farm was, in many ways, his home base. He always returned there over the course of his lifetime, and family members still live there today.

It is easy to see where the two children got their names: Mary Elizabeth was named after her grandmother, and Robert Hyson after his grandfather; both names were picked from Mommy Reese's side of the family.

H. B. Reese (left) with local farm boy (right, name unknown) in 1903

H. B. was not actually fond of farming, and the Frosty Hill Farm was difficult terrain, consisting of many steep hills. Farming was extremely difficult in those days—hard, hot, back-breaking work, often lasting from dawn to dusk. H. B. had to deal with rocks and take extra good care of his animals and equipment. His daughter Mary Elizabeth recounted that she saw her father working the fields with a plow pulled by oxen, which demanded extreme skill and exertion. No one can blame H. B. for not wanting to make this type of farming his life's profession.

H. B. decided to move his family to Ditchley, Virginia, on the western side of Chesapeake Bay, in 1903. His father-in-law made him manager of the fishing operations for his cannery business. H. B. spent the next four years learning about the fishing and canning businesses; both were growing industries at the time.

H. B. would use this knowledge and experience later in his life, canning beans and other vegetables during the summer months when it was too hot to make chocolate candies. He also loved to fish in his later years, buying a fishing lodge at a remote location where he, his family, friends, and employees enjoyed some time off.

While the Reese family lived in Ditchley, their son John Manifold was born, on May 18, 1904. Anna Alfreda soon followed on April 12, 1906.

Mary Elizabeth recounted how, at the age of five, she saw her mother use a wooden store box as a playpen for her newborn baby sister, Anna. Mommy Reese sometimes took the children out on a rowboat for a tour of the local waterways. Supposedly, she put the younger children into a large wash basket for additional safety while in the boat. Mary Elizabeth also remembered vividly how disaster struck when their house caught fire and burned to the ground. Everything was lost except a buffet cabinet from the dining area. A neighboring family by the name of Carter gave the Reeses a place to stay until another house was built.

H. B. lived in Ditchley for four years. He then moved his family back to the Frosty Hill Farm where he worked the land for several more years. At this point, they had four children. They added to that number with the birth of Edward Irons, named after a doctor; he was born February 10, 1908. Next came Marjorie Marie on February 4, 1910, followed by Ralph Collins on November 24, 1911.

With seven children by then living at the Frosty Hill Farm, along with all of the adults, there was not nearly enough space; but the family had plenty of support. H. B.'s father-in-law and other relatives owned several farms within a ten-mile radius of them.

H. B. was just thirty-two years old when he decided to move to Woodbine, a town also in York County, Pennsylvania. He took over farming the land and had several dairy cows for milking. The milk money was used to buy groceries at his father-in-law's store in Bridgeton, which was located just down a dirt road from the farm, next to a creek. During an interview, Mary Elizabeth recounted how Grandpa Hyson always gave them more groceries than milk money could legitimately provide.

Again, thanks to the start his father-in-law gave him and the support along the way, H. B. would end up using his work experience in dairy farming and the cannery business later in his career. Dairy farming eventually brought him to Hershey, Pennsylvania, where he went to work for Milton S. Hershey before beginning his own candy business years later.

With so many children in the family, mischief was bound to occur. Mary Elizabeth tells how she was hanging clothes outside on the clothesline one day when, out of the corner of her eye, she saw a fluffy blanket fall from the second-story porch, to the ground below. Amazingly, the blanket kept on moving after it landed on the ground—turned out to be her little brother, Ralph Collins. He must have been crawling around on the porch and had fallen, but he was not harmed in any way—thanks to the fluffy blanket material.

After the family moved to Woodbine, two more children were born. Helen Grace arrived on November 12, 1913. And Clara Louise (usually known as Louise) followed on September 6, 1915.

With the older children getting ready to enter high school, the family moved to Shrewsbury, also in York County. H. B. took a job in a factory in New Freedom, Pennsylvania. They lived in a house that was almost ready to fall down. Mary Elizabeth admitted that, as a teenager, she was ashamed to live in that house because other girls she knew all seemed to live in large, gorgeous homes.

Opportunity

In 1916, H. B. read an employment ad placed in the local newspaper (the York *Gazette*) by Milton Hershey. He was looking to hire people who could manage and operate his numerous dairy farms. The milk was used to make the milk chocolate needed for Hershey's candies. Little did H. B. know that this opportunity would eventually give him the inspiration to start his own candy business.

H. B. applied for the job with Milton Hershey, and when he went to Hershey for the interview, he took his daughter Mary Elizabeth with him. She was only fifteen years old at the time.

Mary Elizabeth had pleasant memories of the trip with her father to Hershey, traveling by train and a trolley. This was a very impressive trip for the young woman who had grown up in rural areas and had not seen cities even as large as Harrisburg and Hershey. When they arrived in Hershey, she was impressed with the newly constructed streets and the beautiful Hershey Bank and Trust building.

The recently constructed bank building had a very impressive architectural design for those days. It had opened in 1914 and was part of the Hershey town square, the center of attention, located at the corner of West Chocolate and Park Avenues. It had been constructed with red Lancaster brick and Vermont marble trimmings, and it sat upon a base of North Carolina granite. The main entrance had two ionic pillars, and broad granite steps rose to the second story, supporting marble cornices. The roof included a skylight made of ornate stained glass, which provided natural daylight to the floors below.

The city of Hershey (what is really Derry Township) was progressing well by this time. Milton Hershey's dream of an industrial utopian city was under way. The attractive design helped to inspire people to live virtuous, peaceful lives. Everything was new and clean, with artfully landscaped parks, broad avenues, neoclassical buildings, statues, and many other public decorations.

Hershey Park became a place for workers to relax and enjoy life with their families. So it was only natural for the experience to make a big impression on Mary Elizabeth and H. B., who had a growing family to feed and clothe.

The trip paid off, because in 1917 Milton hired H. B. to work as a dairyman at the farm named Twenty-Eight "A". This farm was next to Spring Creek, just off Crest Lane, between Meadow Lane and Golf Road. The farmhouse is no longer standing. We can see where the dairy farm used to be, next to the bend along Spring Creek, but the barn was torn down to make room for housing units for the industrial school.

Moving his family to Hershey was a major undertaking for H. B. His oldest son, Robert, had developed a strong bond with his grandparents since he had never lived far from them during his young life. H. B.'s father-in-law, Robert Bortner Hyson, decided to allow his grandson to live with them, and so Robert Reese was excluded from his family's move. Grandpa Hyson was partial to his namesake, and Little Robert was fortunate to get some hands-on training working in his grandfather's country store.

Robert toted bags of mail from Grandpa Hyson's store to the train station, located on the other side of Muddy Creek, and the agent there taught him how to use the telegraph system. Robert was a quick learner: the agent soon hired him as the full-time telegraph operator. This was not a bad job for a young teenager. Frequent trains ran between Baltimore and York on the "Ma and Pa" railroad, named for Maryland and Pennsylvania. During this time, many farmers shipped their animals and produce via trains. Many goods had to travel in wooden boxes; in addition to his responsibilities as the telegrapher, Robert became adept at crating items that needed to go on the train.

While Little Robert was living with his grandfather, H. B. had moved the rest of his family to Hershey and started working on the diary farm, milking the cows twice a day and running the operation. During the hot summer days, Mary Elizabeth sometimes walked into town to get special treats, such as pie à la mode—chocolate crème pies with homemade vanilla ice cream. Hershey seemed like a dream place to her. Meanwhile H. B. traveled about Hershey and did his work routinely, until he heard that Milton Hershey was making about seventy-five dollars a minute. This gave H. B. inspiration to start his own candy business.

Apparently, Milton Hershey liked H. B.'s work. In 1918 Milton asked H. B. to help manage his experimental dairy farm, called the Round Barn. The Round Barn used to stand on the south side of Airport Road, also known as Hershey Park Drive, near the former Milton High School unit that presently houses the Hershey Partnership offices; this is close to the road leading to the Hotel Hershey. The Round Barn is no longer there because a fire burned it to the ground many years ago. At the time when H. B. worked there, he was responsible for 105 Holstein cows and six milking machines. The Round Barn had just received new milking machines, which were much more efficient than milking the cows by hand. A silo sat in the middle of the barn, which made it easy to pitch hay, and the cows were set up into two rows. Even as young as Ralph Collins Reese was (about seven years of age), his father made it a family endeavor, and had him working in the Round Barn.

One day, Milton Hershey stopped by, saw little Ralph there, and asked him, "What do you do?" Ralph replied, "I carry the buckets in," gesturing toward the empty buckets that would be hooked up to the milking machines. Milton Hershey was impressed by the boy and his father. The two businessmen eventually became unusually good friends.

Young folk often hear stories from parents about how tough things were "back in the old days." However, H. B. and several of his children (Mary Elizabeth, Robert Hyson, and John Manifold) awoke at two in the morning and walked several miles from dairy farm Twenty-Eight "A" to the Round Barn; then they started to milk the cows around four o'clock. When the children finished milking, they had to walk to school—and arrive on time. They did their work while wearing the same clothes they wore during the day in school; according to Mary Elizabeth, they did not have time to change.

Eventually, H. B. was able to move his family to a small house located right next to the Round Barn. Frances Turner was born at this house on April 1, 1918.

Milton Hershey used to stop by the farm about every two weeks. This was his experimental dairy farm, in which he was seeking new approaches to animal treatment and milk production; but in 1919, Hershey found the barn too expensive to maintain and decided to close it down.

H. B. needed to feed his family, and he realized he had to make something happen. Ultimately, he decided to establish a company that would manufacture high-grade candies in a town located close to Hershey. Near the end of 1919, he formed a little business that operated as the R&R Candy Company (probably named for H. B. and John Reese), in Hummelstown, Pennsylvania. He initially began manufacturing chocolate almonds and raisins from a small building known as the canning factory and was able to sell these candies in many of the local stores. The Hummelstown *Sun* gave him some great press coverage and urged local residents to support the new business. A November 28, 1919 advertisement for the company read, "Our goods are on sale at all Hummelstown stores. Ask for them and patronize home industry when buying your Christmas candies."

H. B. knew he needed high-quality manufacturing equipment in order to boost the potential of the candy business so, in January 1920, he decided to raise money by issuing stock in a newly formed company called the Superior Chocolate and Confectionery Company. By May 1920, he was able to capitalize the company with twenty-five thousand dollars and used that money to order manufacturing machinery.

The *Sun* reported that, on May 21, 1920, "Mr. Reese is a practical candy maker and has been operating successfully in a small way for some time. The output of the factory will be greatly increased with the modern machinery and business methods installed, and will be a great addition to Hummelstown's business interest." By September 1920, the machinery arrived, and the company appeared ready to begin operations.

Though H. B. made a strong effort to start a new candy company, the business failed. He decided to move his family to row housing in Spring Grove, Pennsylvania, where he took a job in a local paper mill owned by W. L. Glatfelter. H. B. was going through hard times and had to scramble to keep his head above water. After working a shift in the paper mill, he went to a second job, working as a butcher, and then to yet another as a salesman for what was supposed to be the first oil burner. He even did some canning of vegetables on the side.

H. B. was under considerable pressure because he and Blanche had yet another baby on the way, and he only stayed in Spring Grove from September to December 1920. His father-in-law was able to provide financial help to the family. H. B. must have convinced him that Hershey was the place he could make a living, because Grandpa Hyson bought a house in Hershey at 18 East Areba Avenue for about three thousand dollars and gave it to his son-in-law for his beloved grandchildren. Rose Amos was born there January 16, 1921.

After moving so frequently for the previous six years, having his own home in Hershey was a huge relief for H. B. Maintaining a home for a family as large as his had become was difficult enough, and moving them often had been an even greater strain.

H. B. and his second eldest son John soon found jobs in the shipping room at Milton Hershey's main plant in the center of town. They both worked hard to put food on the table and clothe the rest of the family.

Family members have considerable respect for Uncle John. He had to quit grade school early because H. B. needed help making enough money so the family could survive. John was the kind of person who was very direct and "pulled no punches," high praise among the blue-collar Pennsylvania workers.

Eventually, H. B. was promoted to foreman at the plant. The younger children helped the family as well; Ralph, for instance, sold newspapers (the *Evening News* and the Harrisburg *Telegraph*) near Hershey's chocolate plant and a trolley car stop, and he also had a paper route. Most days, Milton

Hershey bought a newspaper from him for two cents; he would give Ralph a dime and tell him to keep the change. Those eight extra cents in 1921 were worth at least eighty-eight cents today and made Ralph a happy youngster. At the end of a week, he had the equivalent of four or five bonus dollars burning in his pocket.

Vision

There were now eleven children, and H. B. continued to work toward his dream. He started to make candy in the basement of the house. Even though he was working at Milton Hershey's factory, he still needed extra money to feed his ever-growing family. H. B. had already started to form a business relationship with Milton Hershey and had started two candy companies in Hummelstown, so it was only natural for this entrepreneur to begin yet another venture.

Milton Hershey did not lose any business to H. B. because H. B. was buying his chocolate from him. In addition, Hershey was sympathetic toward the young family man and wanted to encourage him. He took a liking to H. B., possibly because he saw how hard the man worked and that he was persistent in his efforts to do his best.

H. B.'s son Robert was still living with his grandfather, and Mary Elizabeth was now twenty years old. She graduated valedictorian from Hershey's Consolidated School and moved to Philadelphia to major in home economics at Temple University. Robert was a supportive brother; he sent money to Mary Elizabeth to help defray the cost of her college education.

It was standard practice at 18 East Areba Avenue to have two children sleeping in each bed, with two beds per bedroom. In addition to having nine children living in the house, H. B.'s mother and her sister still lived with the family. Two additional male borders lived there as well.

While at Frosty Hill Farm, H. B. had met a young man by the name of Ralph Smith (nicknamed "Smitty") who only lived about a mile from the farm. Smitty had gone to school with some of the Reese boys when they were younger, and one day he came to Hershey to visit the family. He ended up renting one of the rooms in the house and soon started to work for H. B. In all, Smitty would go on to work for the Reese family for forty-eight years. Another fellow rented a room in the house as well, a man known by the children as Mr. Bender. H. B. had met Bender at a local market in Harrisburg, Pennsylvania.

As soon as he had enough money to buy the ingredients for his enterprise, H. B. had started making candy in the basement of his house. His son Ralph recounted having to hustle to sell quarter-pound bags of after-dinner peppermints, sometimes door-to-door, for ten cents a bag. H. B. cooked this candy on the stove in the kitchen until it was like taffy. He would then put it on a marble slab to cool. Once it cooled, he hung it on a hook in the dining room and pulled it like taffy into strips. He then cut it with scissors to make the individual candies. Often, the children would assist in cutting the strips, but space was tight so only a few were able to help at any one point.

Marjorie Marie sold bags of candy to Hershey's employees as they left the factory, a certain example of Milton Hershey's kind and generous support of the family. Hershey himself had struggled financially in his earlier days, and he not only tolerated but encouraged the practice of dealing peppermints on the front step of his own candy business.

H. B. eventually started to make other kinds of candies in his basement. He devoted countless hours to experimenting with and developing candies that people would buy and enjoy. Sometimes the experimental candies turned hard as a rock, but eventually H. B. got the formula right, and in the meantime he had grown his own sales force of children to go out and sell his product.

One day, Milton Hershey recommended to H. B. that he limit the number of candy varieties he made to just a few of his best. Hershey was only making two candy bars at that time, a milk chocolate and an almond bar, and he was finding great success. Eventually, H. B. decided to take that recommendation to heart.

H. B. made a square candy bar he called the Lizzie, named after his daughter Mary Elizabeth, and a Johnny bar, named after his son John Manifold. Many people loved the taste of these two candy bars. They are no longer in production, but some of us would like to see these two candies on the shelves again someday. Ingredients included fresh grated coconut, caramel, molasses, cocoa butter, and honey. The main difference between the two candies was that the Johnny bar had nuts.

As sales began to increase, as Hershey had predicted they would, H. B. needed more space. He rented the basement of a local restaurant in Hershey, called DeAngelis (since sold and now called Fenicci's). H. B. also found a few other places to make his candies. Local newspapers reported that he made candy in Palmyra, Pennsylvania.

By this point, we can see that H. B. did what he had to do to provide for his large family, but he also had a career dream. He was a very personable man, and he understood what it was like to go through hard times. And, like Milton Hershey, he loved to help those around him; he was a giving person.

Entrepreneurial Genius Confirmed

The candy business was starting to grow, and so was the family. H. B. tried repeatedly to incorporate his business, but times were still tough. Each time he tried, something went awry. A popular phrase used by H. B. to describe the severity of his situation was "going up the spout," meaning that his plans seemed to run the wrong way. Money became so tight he almost had to file for bankruptcy. They say the third time is a charm, and in H. B.'s case it was; in 1923, he was finally able to incorporate his new business as the H. B. Reese Candy Company.

The family was still growing. In 1923, H. B. and Mommy Reese welcomed another daughter, Mildred Jane, and by then things were finally starting to come together for H. B. and his family. With the number of children he had, it was only a matter of time before he named one after himself, which he did in 1924 with Harry Burnett Jr.

Thomas came along in 1926; however, Mildred Jane had died that same year, and Thomas died in 1927. These were tragic losses for H. B. and Mommy Reese, but they could not allow themselves to falter. They had a family of thirteen other children who needed their support, as well as other relatives living with them. Many of the children were entering their twenties, and there were plenty of brothers and sisters around the house to take care of the younger siblings, which certainly helped. H. B. was able to spend more time on building his new candy business.

Mary Elizabeth was amazed by the number of people who lived in the house at East Areba Avenue. By the time she was twenty-five she had moved to Philadelphia, and well into her nineties she remembered how crowded the house was whenever she visited. Up to twenty men, women, and children cohabited there from 1921–26. The 1,885-square-foot house (built in 1900) might have been considered large for that time period, but today four bedrooms and two baths would be too small for so many people.

In 1926, H. B. borrowed money from the Delta National Bank in York County to build his first real factory and a new house at 205 West Caracas Avenue in Hershey. This new home was just two blocks away from the city's chief thoroughfare, Chocolate Avenue, and just down the street from Milton Hershey's main plant.

The new home was a special place for H. B.'s family, for it had sixteen rooms and was conveniently located right next to his privately owned candy factory. Over the years the house and factory would go through many changes. Today, the house and factory are attached and appear to be one building. At one point, though, the first floor of the house served as office space for the candy business.

Charles Richard Reese
205 West Caracas Avenue

After a few years of living in their new home, H. B. and Mommy Reese had a surprise. She was pregnant yet again, and a set of twins—Charles Richard (Dick) and William—arrived on February 11, 1928. Sadly, William died after only nine months. These two children would be the last two of sixteen born into the family; a total of thirteen children would survive into adulthood.

As Charles Richard (Dick) was growing up, he became quite an athlete. An accomplished springboard diver, at a young age Dick entertained thousands of people over the years at Hershey area pools with his diving exhibitions. Dick was much taller than the average springboard diver, and he looked graceful as he performed. Other swimmers left the pool when they knew he was going to dive because they all wanted to watch him. He would barely miss the springboard as he came down to enter the water; a few times, he scraped the back of his legs on the board. In December 2007, two years after his death, WITF-TV in Harrisburg produced a program called "Growing Up in Hershey," which showed, among other memories, clips of Dick's diving.

In addition to Dick's birth, 1928 was the year that H. B. invented the famous REESE'S Peanut Butter Cups. This was also the year in which the entire family gathered for a photograph, which H. B. used on his candy advertisement. I think all of the family members in my generation have this picture on their walls—I know that I certainly do. The REESE'S Peanut Butter Cups would eventually become one of the most widely recognized candies in the world.

H. B. worked hard all his life to provide a decent home for his large family, and the one on Caracas Avenue was worth describing. The first and entry-level floor had a reception room, living room, formal dining room, a den, kitchen, and back dining room, the last of which featured a huge, made-to-order table with chairs and benches. For some meals, at least eighteen people sat around this table, and several others gathered in the other dining room at the same time.

The second floor had five bedrooms, one bathroom, and a sewing room that provided access to the third floor. There were front and back steps from the first floor to the second floor.

The second floor had a laundry chute that went all the way to the basement. Aunt Rose recounted how one day she caught Dick hanging on by his fingernails inside the chute. A fall probably would not have hurt him, but maybe the ride would have if he had hit a jagged edge! Dick told his own stories about the laundry chute, where he said he hid whenever he got in trouble and people were looking for him.

The huge, custom-built wooden box located in the cellar was always full of everyone's dirty laundry. Washing clothes was a nearly full-time operation. The children did their share of laundry duty. Motorized washing machines were not in use during this time period, and usually someone had to tote the cleaned items outside for hanging on lines. The laundry room was well equipped for the time, though, and included two rough showers and a toilet as well. It was also where all the guns and ammo were stashed; they were hung in a large, open gun rack.

The third floor of the house had three bedrooms and a large hallway. The front bedroom contained two double beds shared by Helen Grace, Clara Louise, Frances Turner, and Rose. Many nights the kids had pillow fights, and conversations sometimes lasted well after lights out. Ralph and Edward had the other two bedrooms on the third floor. The rest of the family shared the second-floor bedrooms.

Over the years, Dick told many stories about the house and his life. Being the youngest, the factory and surrounding neighborhood formed his playground. He had many friends he played with in the neighborhood. He affectionately called them the Caracas Avenue Gang, and they were all lifetime friends.

Little children can be so sneaky when they want to be. One of Dick Reese's friends, Dick Schell, recounted how they played hide-and-seek in the plant, not because they really wanted to hide from each other, but because they wanted to stuff their little faces with candy throughout the day. Pictures of Dick often showed him with a knowing grin on his face. Occasionally, the same grin now appears on his grandson Christopher Richard's face.

Aunt Anna was basically a second mother to her younger siblings. She made clothes for them, cleaned, cooked, and was their ever-present "boss." When she and Mommy Reese baked, everyone could smell the goodies throughout the whole house. Of course, we are not talking about one loaf of bread or one pie. Often, they cooked for nearly twenty people. Aunt Mary recounted that they regularly made six loaves of bread per day. The kitchen looked like something we would see in a restaurant. A large butcher-block table sat in the center of the room, many pots and pans hung on hooks from the ceiling, and the stove always had copper cooking pots in the ready position.

With so many siblings, family anecdotes abound. When the children on the third floor had to do their chores one day, Anna told her younger sister Rose to clean the bathroom—and to put a little elbow grease into it! Rose called out to Anna asking her where the elbow grease was kept because she could not find it.

Eventually, Anna and Marjorie graduated from nursing school at the Pennsylvania Hospital in Philadelphia. This was the first hospital in the United States, built around 1751 and founded by Benjamin Franklin and Dr. Thomas Bond to care for the "sick, poor, and insane of Philadelphia." Anna and Marjorie turned out to be excellent nurses; it was not uncommon for nurses to work as much as twelve hours a day.

H. B. bought a truck from Hess Ford, and one day his son John loaded it with his two favorite candies. He drove to York and found a good spot to sell them, next to a busy store. The owner of the store was told by one of the employees that someone was outside selling candies, so she went out to discover what was going on. She asked John who he was and what he was doing. He told her his name and that he was selling Johnny and Lizzie bars.

She had to ask him the difference between the candy bars. John was quick to reply that the difference between a Johnny and a Lizzie was that the Johnny had nuts. She thought he was trying to make an off-color joke and took offense. To this day, our family has a good laugh over these two candy bars, which were very popular at the time.

After several years in business, H. B.'s company added varieties, including some coated with milk chocolate and some with dark chocolate. These candies were placed in two-pound and five-pound boxes. Specially made boxes had fancy holiday designs on them, which caught people's eyes. These decorated boxes have become highly sought after by collectors from all around the world. Some people use them to store various small items in the house; others keep them in glass showcases for prominent display. Many Reese relatives have original candy boxes sitting on their shelves. People currently are paying anywhere from fifty to seventy dollars for an empty box that used to hold chocolate candies.

Here is a brief list of the types of candy that H. B. sold at the time. Every one was simply delicious because they were made with real cocoa butter, cream, fresh grated coconut, and freshly roasted peanuts:

Coconut Cream *	Raisin Clusters *
Butter Cream	Coated Dates *
Peppermint Cream *	Coconut Caramel *
Chocolate Jets *	Nuttees *
Nougat *	Honey Dew Coconut *
Marshmallow-Nut *	REESE'S Peanut Butter Cups *
Peanut Clusters *	Cream Caramel
Marshmallow	Butterscotch

* These twelve candies were also sold in five-pound boxes during the holiday season.

◆ ◆ ◆

Visitors to Hershey frequently ask how REESE'S Peanut Butter Cups were invented. Was it by mistake or by design?

In late 1927, H. B. was delivering some of his candy to a store in Harrisburg, the Bluebird Candy Shop. The owner of the shop was having problems with another supplier who could not keep him supplied with a candy made of peanut butter covered with chocolate. He asked H. B. if he could supply him with something like that. H. B. saw an opportunity and, with considerable persistence, seized it.

Dick recounted that H. B. originally rolled the peanut butter into a small ball and dipped it into chocolate; the peanut butter manufacturing process was easy to automate, and the cup was used to help that process, since it provided a small compartment for each item. The candy was quickly added to the assortment box in 1928.

There is more to this story, though. The type of Reese's own peanut butter distinguished the taste for this candy. Many companies have tried to duplicate it and failed. In fact, the choice of the particular flavor of the peanut butter took place by accident. When H. B. bought new roasting machines to increase his production, the taste of the peanut butter changed. He soon discovered that the old machines had been malfunctioning—they were burning the peanuts. Amused but challenged, H. B. and his crew immediately set out to duplicate the old roasting flavor.

One other ingredient must remain a mystery. Many competitors have tried to duplicate the REESE'S Peanut Butter Cups, but their product sales did not take off. We can only reveal that the flavor of the peanut butter and the type of milk chocolate used make all the difference; further details are secret.

In the early days, each candy was coated by hand on marble slabs that were about thirty-six inches by thirty-six inches, with four women coating candies at each table. John Manifold Reese's son Stanley recently donated one of those old marble slabs to the Hershey Historical Society, a great place to visit. The assorted candies were packed in boxes and sold to department stores for resale by bulk weight.

Candy Easter eggs became very popular, mostly chocolate candies that contained either coconut or peanut butter. The eggs were also sold in half-pound and one-pound sizes and could be decorated with names written on the eggs if so desired.

Aunt Shirley, wife of Harry Burnett Reese Jr., recounted that Milton Hershey and H. B. use to sit on the porch for hours and talk. Hershey would also stop by the factory and run experiments with H. B. One day, when he stopped by the factory, he walked up to Clara Louise and Helen Grace and put his arms around the two of them. He asked H. B. admiringly if the two young ladies were his daughters, which they were. Little did Hershey know that the two girls had come to the factory that day just to meet him; he really made their day! They thought Milton Hershey was a sweetheart.

The Great Depression

In 1928, H. B.'s company started including REESE'S Peanut Butter Cups in its assorted candy line, and this year also happened to be the year before the world took a big economic downturn.

Family legend has it that the sheriff would come walking up to the front door of the house, looking for H. B., but could never find him—as soon as H. B. heard that the sheriff was coming he was out the back door. He would hightail it down to the Frosty Hill Farm and hide there for two or three days.

During those Depression years, the Delta Bank stood by H. B. and saved him from a sheriff's sale more than once. Times were hard back then, and everyone looked out for each other.

H. B. sold his candies in many department stores and little neighborhood grocery stores; however, profits were based upon consignment, and H. B. did not get paid until the candies were actually sold. It took a lot of money to float product in all those stores across the country.

H. B. was his own best salesman. Ralph Collins Reese recounted how he drove H. B. to several small cities on a regular basis: Harrisburg, York, Lancaster, Pottsville, Lebanon, Allentown, Easton, and Reading. In order to promote sales, H. B. set up a special coating table in the front display window of large, downtown department stores and several employees coated the candies in full view of the shoppers passing by.

Displaying the manufacturing process gave potential buyers the opportunity to watch their candies take shape, and inside the store, other employees handed out freshly made samples. The candies were so delicious that just one taste would prompt most customers to purchase candies to take home.

Workers Coating Candy

Times were still tough, and since sales were based on consignment sometimes H. B. did not have enough money to pay his workers at the end of the day. Many employees did not cash their paychecks right away, at least not until H. B. had enough money in the bank to cover them. Rena Renshaw, a former employee, recounted how she once had gone about six weeks without getting paid. The employees understood the situation, trusted H. B., and were loyal to him. They worked for H. B. and allowed him to pay them when he had the money to do so.

Obviously, H. B. made good on paying his employees; but the level of trust was extraordinary. There were times when employees needed their money right away, so H. B. did the best he could. If need be, he would give his employees boxes of candy to take to a customer's store. Sometimes the employees were able to get paid in cash for the candies; other times they were paid with groceries. This says a lot for the people who worked for H. B. and how people did what they had to do to survive.

H. B. Reese walking home

Many people have heard the stories about how Milton Hershey made sure people were employed during the Depression. Here is another. H. B. bought his milk chocolate from Milton Hershey's company. One day, he went over to get a load of milk chocolate; however, a manager told him that he was late on making his payments and would not be extended any more credit. As H. B. was walking home from the Hershey plant, he just happened to meet Hershey himself. After a brief conversation, Hershey went directly to his chief financial officer, John William Seitzinger, and in short order H. B. had the chocolate supply he needed.

John Seitzinger and Andrew Reese

Years later, Hershey's valued employee William Seitzinger would enter our family's life again, when his own grandson John Seitzinger came to work for ReeseWeb, the author's own information security consulting company.

◆ ◆ ◆

The relationship between H. B. and Milton Hershey was strong enough to withstand the trials of the Depression years. They sat on the porch together at the Reese Caracas Avenue plant to, as they said, "shoot the breeze." The men were both entrepreneurs who had several businesses fail before finding success. Each had received help from his relatives during tough times, and they shared interests in diverse topics, such as dairy farming. H. B. was one of Hershey's major customers as well as a kind of protégé, and the men were close friends.

In some ways, however, they were quite different. Hershey and his wife had no children, while H. B. and Mommy Reese had sixteen. Some of Hershey's concern for H. B. may have come from this very distinction.

It is amazing how people worked together during the Depression years. They understood the situation that everyone was in, and many were sympathetic.

A case in point: a telephone pole located outside H. B.'s home had a special sign on it, telling hoboes and the homeless that they could find a meal at this house. H. B. never turned hungry people away. Martha Reed, a former company employee, recounted how H. B. always offered employment to people who were looking for work. H. B. gave everyone a chance. He hired

Rena Renshaw a few months before her sixteenth birthday; she had been turned down for a job at Milton Hershey's company because she was not sixteen yet. If H. B. bent the laws, no one appeared to mind. He knew how hard it was to make a living and was lucky enough to have people help him out as well; he always gave back to the community when and how he could. During these tough times, H. B., John Manifold Reese, Edward Irons Reese, and Ralph Collins Reese often worked without pay.

Aunt Rose recounted the first time her father, H. B., tried to make a five-cent package of REESE'S Peanut Butter Cups. He had a table built with a small chute that was wide enough for a penny cup. He asked her to help him test it out. Rose placed a narrow cellophane bag over the end of the little chute; her father then fed the penny pieces into the chute, and Rose pushed five pieces into the cellophane bag, turned the end under, and put the bag into another box.

H. B. was expert at figuring cost, and he had to calculate how fast a five-cent package could be produced. For all the work that Rose did, still a young girl at the time, her first weekly paycheck netted $8.94. This sounds small but was a fair amount of money in those days. Rose remembers to this day that she used the money to buy herself some new snow pants.

Several former employees recounted how they made twenty-five cents to thirty cents per hour while working for H. B. during those years, a very decent wage. They noted that this pay was approximately five to ten cents more than they could make at comparable jobs. Over time, different unions tried to get into H. B.'s candy company; however, his employees felt that H. B. was fair and paid them good wages. The employees overwhelmingly voted not to have a union; these results speak to the working environment that H. B. provided his employees.

Process in 1935

In 1935, H. B. had sixty-two employees plus his six sons working at the factory. REESE'S Peanut Butter Cups had become quite popular, and the company was soon packaging 120 pieces per box that sold for a penny per cup. These boxes were shipped to various venues, not just department stores. Five-pound boxes went to distributors like Fanny Farmer for inclusion in their own candy assortments. The penny-size peanut butter cups were the candy that helped H. B. burn the mortgages for his house and factory by 1935. This is especially noteworthy since the country was still in the grip of the Great Depression and chocolate was considered a luxury.

H. B. Reese and Associates, 1935

Stanley Reese recounted his understanding of how the peanut butter was made around that time. He was still a young man when the old plant was in operation, but he remembered details from that time period because he had also played there while he grew up. Grade A Number One Spanish runner peanuts were trucked into the plant in 125-pound burlap bags. Three or four strong young men, called the bull gang, unloaded the bags from the trucks. The peanuts were shelled and roasted in the basement of the factory, in a natural gas roaster that looked something like a cement mixer. The time that the peanuts were roasted was critical in order to elicit maximum flavor. After roasting, they were run through a vibrating machine that contained a mesh bottom. The open holes in the mesh allowed the thin, brittle skins, called the hulls, to be separated from the peanuts. The hulls were bagged in burlap and sold to farmers to be mixed in with their cattle feed.

Roasted peanuts then went through a process in which they were thoroughly cleaned and ground. The resulting peanut material was measured and placed in large kettles that fit into large Hobart mixers. Specially made scoops were designed to measure the exact quantities of other ingredients, which were added to the peanut material to make the properly flavored peanut butter. Once two kettles of peanut butter had been mixed, workers deposited the result into a tub, which they wheeled into a cooling room until needed later in the production process. The tubs looked like huge bread pans, the size of bathtubs. This cooling room did not have humidity controls; this type of advanced control was one addition when the company built a newer plant in 1957.

Aunt Rose told how her son Jim played in and near the old factory. He lived at the old house for six years with his mother. Sometimes, Jim took freshly made peanut butter and molded a bunch of it into patties on the curb. H. B. saw Jim doing this one day and gave him a tongue-lashing, "Don't ever let me see you do that again!"

The very next day, Jim was out on the curb making peanut butter patties again. When H. B. heard about it, he proceeded to give the boy another stern scolding: "I thought I told you never to do that again!"

Jim replied, "But you didn't see me!"

Jim was like all the other children: he loved to eat as much candy as he could. He loved it so much that his two front teeth rotted out; however, he was lucky in that they were still only his baby teeth.

John Powell, a former employee, recounted the manufacturing process for creating the peanut butter wedges placed into the REESE'S Peanut Butter Cups. He commented that employees used what looked like two old sausage-stuffer machines mounted on a handmade frame to create the peanut butter wedges. Workers used a spatula cutting tool to remove large chunks of peanut butter from storage tubs, placing the chunks into the top of the sausage-stuffer machines—or what we might more precisely term a peanut butter extruding machine. As the peanut butter came out of a circular spout, a rotating, wire cutting tool sliced the peanut butter into a proportionately sized wedge. The freshly cut wedges were then placed on plywood trays.

Rena Renshaw described the manufacturing process for creating the milk chocolate. She said they had a mixer in which they melted ten-pound cakes of milk chocolate from Milton Hershey's candy company. Using a hatchet, employees chopped up the ten-pound blocks so they would be easier to melt. After that, they poured the melted chocolate into pans placed on the coating tables. Sometimes they had to stir the milk chocolate until it cooled enough to be used to coat the candy. Experienced workers could tell if the chocolate was still too hot because once they placed it into the cups it would turn a shade of white. The temperature of the chocolate had to be just so, or the product would not look right; it still could have a good chocolate taste, but appearance was important, too. Stanley Reese called this process "tempering."

Several young women, sitting around the coating tables, were responsible for coating the candies. Coating without dripping milk chocolate all over the trays required precise focus. Once a tray contained a full set of coated candies, it was placed on a conveyer belt and fed to a cooling system that solidified the candies for about thirty minutes. When it came out of the cooling system, the candies were ready to be packaged. Cooling technology was limited at the time, and air-conditioning was rare. They were only able to use the cooling machine when the inside temperature was below eighty degrees; otherwise, operations came to a halt because they could not cool the candies enough to solidify them. In those years, they did not have packing machines, so everything had to be done by hand. The workers boxed the candy and weighed it. Then the boxes were placed into cartons for shipping.

Factory employees usually received the first two weeks of July off because the seasonal heat made it their slow season. The maintenance people came to the plant to retool or redesign machinery and prepare for the following year.

During the hotter months, H. B. set up a little canning operation for green beans, corn, and tomatoes. He obtained fresh produce from local areas, such as Bachmanville, Hummelstown, Swatara, and the Sponaugle Farm. Migrant workers picked the produce, and were paid by the amount of produce they picked, which was measured by the weight of the produce bags. Once again, perseverance, ingenuity, and relating well to employees helped H. B. succeed.

◆ ◆ ◆

Around the mid-1930s, Mr. Houston, one of H. B.'s salesmen, reported to H. B. that REESE'S Peanut Butter Cups could probably sell without having to be part of the candy assortment. He must have noticed a large demand for them. It did not take long for H. B. to follow up on this suggestion and to sell the cups as single products, separate from the assorted candy boxes.

Aunt Rose described how cartons of candy were placed into a specially made chute that fed product to the delivery dock and trucks. At the bottom of the chute was a track of rollers that had collapsible extensions that could be set up to feed product into trucks. Children in the neighborhood treated the chute like a giant slide on which to play. In today's litigious society, a company surely would forbid this seemingly dangerous practice. But Stanley Reese told stories of how he and others slid down the chute, sometimes atop of waxed paper, and apparently no one was hurt.

School children came by the factory frequently and bought scrap pieces of candy for a fraction of what the candy would cost retail; each of these candies had some deformity that prevented it from being sold as marketable product. Sometimes, the children purchased large bags of scrap pieces. One older man purchased scrap pieces and sold them at area flea markets. Selling scrap pieces was an easy way to recoup some of the money spent to make the candy.

In general, H. B. was a good-natured man and was friendly toward everyone; he rarely held a grudge. However, he could apply reasonable discipline to protect his company. Occasionally, critical machinery broke down; sometimes from wear and tear but other times due to deliberate actions by one or two employees who wanted an excuse to get out of work. One employee, in particular, always wanted to go fishing; somehow the hatchet used to break up the blocks of milk chocolate "accidentally" dropped into a machine, breaking it. Everything came to a screeching halt; it typically took the whole day to fix the broken machine. This eventually became a quick way to get fired.

Machinery maintenance was always a concern. The business was still developing, and money for repairs was scarce. Fortunately, H. B.'s son John could fix just about anything.

H. B. Reese

As generous and considerate as he was, H. B. kept a keen eye on his business. Aunt Rose told a story about one instance in which someone was stealing money that was lying around in the office. H. B. asked John to drill a hole in the floor above the office space and watch the room to see who came in and took the money. They caught the thief in short order. If the person had asked for help, H. B. doubtless would have stepped up; but he could not abide theft.

Fishing Lodge and Home Life

After all the years of hard work, H. B. deserved some enjoyment in his life. Around 1935, he built a fishing lodge in Wachapreague, Virginia, located on the eastern shore of Chesapeake Bay. Wachapreague is on the ocean side, south of Chincoteague.

The term *lodge* might be misleading. The house was huge, featuring thirteen bedrooms, a large dining/living room, kitchen, and a screened-in porch that ran the full length of the house. The first floor had five bedrooms and two baths, and the second floor had eight smaller bedrooms and two more baths. There was also an outdoor shower.

Considering that H. B. grew up on the Frosty Hill Farm where he got to fish whenever he wanted in the bubbling creek next to his house (the place where a fishing derby is still held every year), and the experience he received while managing fishing operations at his father-in-law's cannery—it is easy to understand why H. B. was an avid fisherman his whole life.

Fishing Lodge, 1945

Brooks Parker was hired as captain for H. B.'s thirty-two-foot cabin cruiser, named *Rosemary* after his youngest and oldest daughters, Rose and Mary.

The Rosemary Cabin Cruiser

Reese employees were welcome to vacation at the fishing lodge. They could eat and fish for one dollar a day, a great benefit and just one example of the strong relationship H. B. had with his employees. On some weekends, as many as thirty-five guests stayed at the lodge. A large scow, towed behind the *Rosemary*, carried the overflow of people—which boat caught more fish is hard to know.

The Scow in Tow

Dick Reese had a delightful if unusual sense of humor, and he always laughed at his own jokes. One favorite joke, which he may have learned at the fishing lodge, included this definition: "What is a fisherman? It is a jerk waiting for a jerk on the other end!"

Many people have shared fond memories of the food at the lodge. Considering the size of H. B.'s family, preparing larger quantities of food was a regular routine for the cooking crew. The meals were fantastic and included such things as fresh sea trout, croakers, flounder, crab cakes, and fried chicken. Family members have said the clam fritters were the best anywhere; no one has duplicated that taste since. There was also plenty of fresh corn bread.

Charles Richard Reese and Ralph Smith

A lovely woman whom everyone called Aunt Susan was the cook at the lodge for several years. Later, Mayme Shields became the cook, and in the winter months she came to Hershey to cook and clean; she was a big help at the Hershey home. The cooks frequently fixed H. B. his favorite breakfast while at the fishing lodge: poached trout served with brown butter and black pepper.

Rose spent much of her summer teenage life at the Wachapreague fishing lodge and had great times there. One family picture shows Rose taking a look at a fairly large sea turtle with her brother Dick. Smiles are everywhere in photos from the fishing lodge.

Charles Richard Reese and Rose Amos (Reese) Rippon

H. B. had a seven-passenger Buick that he used to drive to the lodge. When Rose turned sixteen years old, this was the car that she got to drive; back then, that was a real treat for a teenager. When H. B. fell asleep in the back seat of the car during a drive one day, she knew that he finally trusted her at the wheel.

◆ ◆ ◆

Christmas back at home in Hershey was a big attraction for the family, as well as many of the family's friends. A large decorated tree sat just inside the front door in the reception room. Everyone bought each other a gift, even if it was only a ten-cent pack of bobby pins. Standard practice was to open all gifts on Christmas Eve. Christmas dinners were normally served with *two* twenty-five-pound turkeys.

Mary Elizabeth recounted how one year they had over forty-two people at the Christmas dinner. Luckily, the house had two dining rooms, but all of the dirty pots, pans, silverware, and dishes had to be washed by hand. After the meal, H. B. announced that this was going to be the last year for such a family dinner—way too many people—from then on, individual family branches would need to have their own dinners in their own homes. It should be noted here that, as of 2007, there were 178 descendents from H. B. and Mommy Reese, of which 155 were still living.

Over the years, H. B. mastered the art of making oyster stew, just as he succeeded in everything else he took an interest in. He would get a barrel of fresh oysters from Baltimore and shuck them on a special table he designed. Often, he used two huge pots to make his stew, always slowly heating the oysters in a separate pan with lots of creamy butter and then adding them to the milk and cream. During the cold months, he sometimes invited employees to come over to the house, which was next to the factory, and enjoy his freshly made batches of oyster stew.

Mommy Reese was well known for her homemade bread and rolls and baked several batches a week. The family never ate store-bought bread, and most foods served in the house were made from scratch.

When Mommy Reese was around thirteen years old, she had an eye infection; for the rest of her life, she could not see very well. Mary Elizabeth mentioned that Mommy Reese had choroiditis; her eyes were filled with black spots. Her ability to see only got worse as she aged. She was able to distinguish the value of coins just by feeling them. In some people's eyes, Mommy Reese was a saint to give birth to sixteen babies: no one ever heard her complain. Her contribution and support to her children and the success of her husband were monumental.

World War II

World War II called upon everyone in our nation to lend his or her support, and sugar quickly became a rationed commodity. The sales pipeline for REESE'S Peanut Butter Cups was large and showed continuous growth potential to this point. With sugar rationing and the various product sales being what they were, H. B. decided to focus on his bestselling candy, the peanut butter cups, whose production was the easiest to automate. This decision followed Milton Hershey's old recommendation of focusing on the best products only. By early in the war, H. B. discontinued production of boxes of assorted chocolates altogether.

By then, the first five-cent cup had been manufactured. Plant automation allowed larger pieces to be produced as fast as a penny piece, with less sugar per ounce, and this helped to boost sales and meet growing product demand.

REESE'S Peanut Butter Cups were gaining ever-expanding recognition. Ralph Collins Reese recounted that, when wrapping machines and vending machines were placed into production, the business doubled in size just about every four years.

When *Fortune* magazine did a cover story on Milton Hershey in the early 1940s, it was noted that he reached into his desk drawer and presented a box of REESE'S Peanut Butter Cups as his gift to the *Fortune* reporter, saying, "Take these delicious treats home for your wife and family."

The success of H. B.'s candy company added to the bottom line of Hershey's milk chocolate sales, keeping Hershey happy; and many servicemen and women loved the product, which they could conveniently eat almost anywhere.

Poppy & Mommy Reese, 1950
Celebrating their 50th Wedding Anniversary

A Great Man's Legacy

During and after World War II, H. B.'s candy company experienced growing demand for his peanut butter cups. He began to envision a modern, air-conditioned plant equipped with state-of-the-art, mass production line machinery. His vision was to produce candy using as much automated machinery as possible. By this time, H. B. had one guiding principal that he made sure everyone knew: "One product only … the best."

H. B.'s sons were stepping up to the plate to manage the business, giving H. B. a well-deserved break. After staying in hotel efficiencies in Florida for a period of time, H. B. bought a house in Vero Beach.

1808 20th Avenue, Vero Beach, Florida

Rose Rippon's son Jim recounted a trip to West Palm Beach, Florida, which he took with H. B. when Jim was a young boy. Jim was allowed to bring a neighborhood friend with him, and H. B. brought along a coworker to help with the driving on the long trip from Pennsylvania. The two men sat in the front while the boys talked and played in the back seat of the car. H. B. loved to make short stops along the way, for food or to enjoy the scenery.

H. B. enjoyed visiting local markets; he would purchase fresh oranges and had a squeezer in the car to use to make orange juice on the spot. During one such stop, the two boys had to go to the bathroom, so they hopped out of the car to use the facility. H. B. did not realize that the boys were gone and soon drove off. When they came out of the bathroom, the boys saw that the car was gone. H. B. drove down the road for about half an hour before he wondered about the silence of the back seat. He quickly turned the car around and drove back to the last stop where he found the two boys waiting for him. When they got to West Palm Beach, they stayed in a local hotel that had suites with two bedrooms; H. B. would end up staying at this hotel often until he eventually bought his house at Vero Beach.

H. B. expected all of his sons to work in his business. Six sons would eventually take over the management of the plant. They divided the duties: three of them—Robert, Ralph, and Harry Burnett Jr.—managed the corporate side. The other three—John, Edward, and Charles Richard (Dick)—took over plant operations. In addition, after World War II, the boys had hired George Duval McClees as office manager; by 1956, George had been promoted to assistant to the president of the company.

Robert learned a lot about business as a young man from his experiences while working for his grandpa, Robert Bortner Hyson. John learned by working at H. B.'s side, starting at the dairy farms and earning his stripes at Milton Hershey's shipping department at a very young age. Ralph attended Beckley's Business College in Harrisburg, Pennsylvania. Edward shared many of the same working experiences as John, at a young age as well. Harry Burnett Jr. (who was injured in a car crash, which kept him from graduating from high school with his class and earning his diploma until a later year) went to work for the candy company, and also attended schools to study office automation. Charles was afforded the opportunity to go to Babson College near Boston, Massachusetts. Several of the Reese girls also got to go to technical schools and college as well, which was not so common at the time.

New Plant under Construction, 1956

By the 1950s, the time had come for expansion. H. B. had a vision for his company and a plan for its execution. He expected to travel from Florida to Hershey, to see the new factory as it was being built; however, he became quite ill, and his doctor in Florida would not allow him to travel.

◆ ◆ ◆

H. B. died of a heart attack in West Palm Beach, Florida, one week before his seventy-seventh birthday, in May 1956. He and Mommy Reese are buried in the Hershey cemetery, not far Milton Hershey's grave.

◆ ◆ ◆

Although H. B. did not get the opportunity to see his new factory being built, his six sons had grown up in the business and were completely running the operation by this time.

New Plant under Construction, 1956

H. B. left the business in the care of his six sons because he felt his girls should be taken care of by their husbands. People might not think this way today, but it was a commonly held view of the time.

Mommy Reese and Six Sons, 1963

H. B. had left his candy company to his six sons, but it is important to note that the six boys each contributed to a trust fund to help make sure their sisters were taken care of financially.

Mommy Reese and Six Daughters, 1963

Though none of H. B.'s six sons had any college education that applied specifically to the candy industry, they earned the honor and respect they received. In 1957, they moved the company production operations from 205 West Caracas Avenue to a new facility just west of Hershey, now called Reese Avenue. They modernized the factory with the latest technology, which would support the growth of the company for many years to come. And they further expanded the business after they moved the factory, from approximately ten million dollars annually in 1950 to over fourteen million dollars by 1957. Records show that, by 1962, they recorded twenty-six million dollars in sales, with a projection of thirty million by 1963.

It took a lot of knowledge and expertise to put the new machinery in place at the factory. The brothers brought in qualified engineers from well-known colleges around the country; but, occasionally, natural-born talent trumps education. John had a remarkable ability to fix things, and there were times when those people with advanced degrees could only marvel at his knack. Family members say he could repair sewing machines when he was eight years old. The other brothers had many talents as well, including expert business acumen.

New Plant under Construction, 1956

The new factory was formally dedicated on November 30, 1957. Many photographs—including aerial shots—and considerable movie footage show the plant under construction, next to a water tower that has since been torn down. When the factory was built, it was the largest single-purpose product line factory in the United States.

New Plant under Construction, 1956

The new plant was 136 feet in width and 425 feet in length, constructed on eight acres of land. It enclosed a spacious ninety-six thousand square feet of floor space divided into offices, a manufacturing department, storage and shipping areas, as well as a large cafeteria for the employees.

The New Plant Nears Completion, 1957

The Reese Family considers this plant to be a living monument to H. B. (Poppy) Reese and his accomplishments.

Process in 1957

The factory had been fitted with state of the art manufacturing equipment. Staying away from the details of machinery models and manufacturer names, the manufacturing process went something like this:

In order to make a good quality product, about twenty-one tons of "Grade A Number One runner peanuts" were used per day. There are many grades of peanuts, grown in different parts of the world, and after considerable study, the company chose to continue using these peanuts in the new factory because of their taste, which, by then, was a hallmark of the REESE'S Peanut Butter Cups. The raw shelled peanuts were fed into hoppers of a pneumatic cleaner located in the lower level of the plant, which removed light trash by air stream technology; the heavier peanuts dropped as the air lifted out light trash, such as paper and wood sticks; additionally, peanuts were conveyed to a rotary screen that provided mechanical separation to remove larger sticks or strings not caught by the other cleaner.

Next, workers fed the peanuts into recirculation roasters where collectors helped to remove loose hulls and thus were assured of a smudge-free roast. After roasting them, workers emptied the peanuts into huge cooling trays, and a manual raking process helped the cooling process. A cooler header and fan assembly located in the end of the tray sucked the air from the top of the peanut pile down through the nuts and into the opening leading to the fan assembly.

Roasted Peanuts

A blancher then helped separate the peanuts, using a friction method to loosen the skins and for further skin debris removal. Then, another blanched nut cleaner with a special patented boot removed metal, stones, and heavy foreign matter that might otherwise damage grinding machinery.

Low velocity air gently forced the peanuts through vertical riser pipes to storage bins located in the penthouse above the peanut butter mills. They were then ground to a desired texture and weighed into batches. Other ingredients—such as salt, sugar, and dextrose—were added in properly measured quantities and thoroughly mixed before taking the whole to a cooling room.

As the peanut butter was needed, batches were placed into extruding machines. The machinery was specially designed for easy cleaning, a big concern when working with the peanut butter manufacturing process.

The Production Line

In another part of the factory, employees daily blended about sixty thousand pounds of milk chocolate, from Milton Hershey's company, melting it in holding tanks. The melted chocolate was then piped into temperature control systems and special depositors.

In the final production stage, separately processed peanut butter, milk chocolate, and glassine cups were brought together for assembly of the finished product.

The company made its own glassine crinkle cups, used to hold the product. The cups were placed into metal trays that had holes spaced out to hold them in exact position under the extruders and depositor nozzles. These trays were moving on a conveyer system, synchronized with the extruders and depositors. The tray full of cups moved under the depositors first, and each cup received a specific amount of tempered milk chocolate, which covered the bottom. A few feet farther down the line, extruders perfectly placed a small, round piece of peanut butter into the cup, on top of the milk chocolate. A second set of depositors placed another portion of tempered milk chocolate on top. The cups were then routed through a cooling tunnel where the milk chocolate was allowed to solidify.

Finally, a single-flow manufacturing line directed the product to wrapping, packing, and the storage and shipping room.

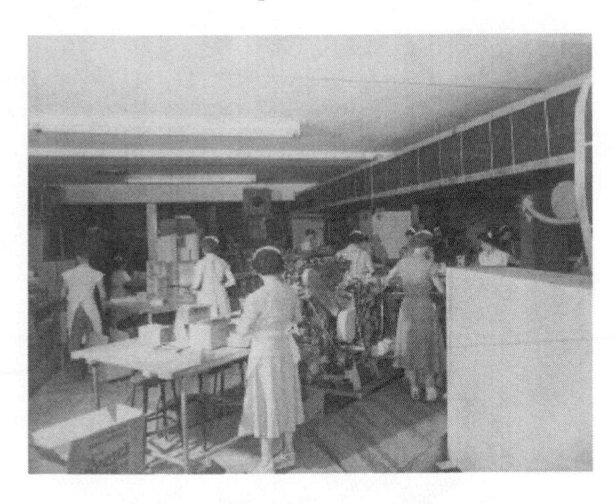

Packaging

By now the business employed several people who had been with the company for decades. Ralph Smith was the chief candy cook for the company; he lived with the Reese family for many years and appears in many of the family photos. He worked for the candy company for forty-eight years, until 1971, retiring one year before his death. George McClees was hired in 1945; by 1960, he had been promoted to the position of executive vice president. He would eventually become vice president and general manager from 1963–74. These were just two of the many people who were loyal to the company over an extended period of time.

With brothers running the company, personnel conflicts occasionally arose. One of the brothers might fire an employee, only to learn that another brother hired the same person back to work for him. This happened more than once.

Ralph "Smitty" Smith

Merger

By the late 1950s, the family had created two companies: the H. B. Reese Candy Company and Reeco, Inc., which held real estate. The list of family corporate officers was as follows:

Robert Hyson Reese	Chairman, H. B. Reese Candy Company
John Manifold Reese	President, H. B. Reese Candy Company
Edward Iron Reese	No title listed in merger document.
Ralph Collins Reese	Secretary, H. B. Reese Candy Company
Harry Burnett Reese Jr.	President, Reeco, Inc.
Charles Richard Reese	Secretary, Reeco, Inc.

The Reese Brothers, 1963

Back Row: John Manifold Reese and Robert Hyson Reese

Front Row: Charles Richard Reese, Edward Irons Reese. Ralph Collins Reese, and Harry Burnett Reese Jr.

◆ ◆ ◆

On April 12, 1963, the six surviving Reese brothers announced the merger of the H. B. Reese Candy Co. with the Hershey Chocolate Corporation. H. B. had often quipped, "If Mr. Hershey can make a million dollars selling his candy, I should at least make a living selling mine." H. B. fortunately did a little better than make a living, and now the two corporate giants would unite.

In the 1950s, H. B.'s candy company was ranked as one of the largest on the east coast, with sales achieving approximately ten million dollars annually; his company was the second largest buyer of Milton Hershey's chocolate (Mars was the largest buyer). At the time of the merger, there were three lines producing REESE'S Peanut Butter Cups.

Several publications stated that H. B.'s company sold for $23.3 million dollars. On June 26, 1963, 666,316 shares of Hershey's stock were documented at $34.50 per share; this equates to $22,987,902.00 and was paid to the newly formed company, H. B. Reese Candy Co., a newly formed

Delaware Corporation. The Hershey stock had actually gone down in value from a reported value of 36 1/8, as reported by the *Patriot* newspaper, on April 12, 1963.

The merger was completed on July 2, 1963, at the library of McNees, Wallace & Nurrick, on the twelfth floor of the Commerce Building in Harrisburg, Pennsylvania. Essentially, the H. B. Reese Candy Company was sold by the six brothers and officially became a subsidiary of the Hershey Chocolate Corporation.

◆ ◆ ◆

Why did the six brothers decide to sell the business? A few texts suggest that family members felt the business had outgrown their ability to run it, and that was the reason why other companies started to look at them for acquisition. However, this view runs contrary to the fact that the brothers knew their abilities well in advance of this merger; they grew up working in this business, some for over forty years by this time.

They also hired people to help them run the business. Family owned companies had done this sort of thing before—this is nothing new to any industry. In fact, George D. McClees was hired back in 1945, many years before the company ever considered a merger with Hershey Chocolate Corporation, and he was the plant manager from 1963–74. Obviously, there was enough talent in the company before the merger to run the business.

Some oral histories suggest that the six brothers were not getting along. Internal disagreements among brothers are not unusual, but they were minor and not the reason for selling the business. The brothers got along so well that each wanted the other to not only be successful, but happy too.

One might think the cause was the number of relatives who were growing up and wanted to be in the business. True, several family members were interested. But in the end, this was not the reason for the sale.

Actually, the brothers had worked in the industry for a very long time. Robert was sixty-one years old and had been with the candy company from 1937–63. John was fifty-nine years old and had worked with H. B. and the candy business from 1919–63. Edward had worked in the company since childhood as well, 1923–63. They had lived through some pretty tough times over the years. The three oldest boys were ready to get out of the business. Ralph was an easy-going fellow; it did not matter to him whether they kept the company or sold it. Initially, only the two younger brothers—Harry Burnett Jr. and Charles—preferred not to sell. The two oldest brothers owned twenty percent of the business each; the other four brothers owned fifteen percent each. This may have been a reason for the youngest brothers' early discontent with talk of selling.

It is likely that many companies were interested in acquiring the candy company. Samuel F. Hinkle, president of Hershey Chocolate Corporation, actually had his eye on the company for years, and he ultimately was able to structure a deal that all six brothers were willing to accept. The older brothers were able to retire, and others invested their monies from the sale. Dick went to Niagara Falls, Ontario, and helped found many businesses there, including: Michael's Inn, the Skylon Tower, and Reese's Country Inn, which was located in the bottom of his rather large house. He eventually moved to Vancouver, British Columbia, and opened a restaurant there called Reese's.

◆ ◆ ◆

Like Milton Hershey, H. B. Reese was a visionary, and the candy he invented is known and liked throughout the world. On the Internet, you can find many fans for REESE'S Peanut Butter Cups. Ebay sells all kinds of Reese memorabilia. YouTube has a number of related video clips that are fun to watch. People from all over the world submit their videos, proving that people have their own ways of enjoying the treat.

H. B. was fond of saying, "If you make a product that both young and old enjoy, then your potential customers are limited only by the number of people on earth." How thrilled he would be today to know that children and grown-ups don't say, "I'll have a peanut butter cup," but instead say, "Give me a Reese's."

Poppy & Mommy Reese

About the Author

Photographed by: Valerie Thompson

Andrew Reese is the grandson of H. B. Reese, founder of REESE'S Peanut Butter Cups. As family historian, he accumulated the most accurate accounting of his family's legacy. Born and currently living in Hershey, Pennsylvania, the author's research and family connections provide a unique look into the history of a famous inventor. Visit his web site, http://www.ReeseWeb.com/, for more information.

Bibliography

Interviews:

Hinkle, Samuel. June 30, 1975. Interview 91OH01 by Ken Bowers. Hershey Community Archives Oral History Collection, Hershey, PA.

Lauzon, C. Louise. March 2, 1992. Interview 920H08 by Monica Spiese. Hershey Community Archives Oral History Collection, Hershey, Pennsylvania.

Pearson, Mary E. (Reese). April 11, 1991. Interview 910H07 by Monica Spiese. Hershey Community Archives Oral History Collection, Hershey, PA.

Powell, John. September 9, 1993. Interview 93OH11 by Brian Lauzon. Hershey Community Archives Oral History Collection, Hershey, PA.

Reese, Ralph C. April 26, 1991. Interview 910H10 by Monica Spiese. Hershey Community Archives Oral History Collection, Hershey, PA.

Renshaw, Rena. August 7, 1993. Interview 930H12 by Brian Lauzon. Hershey Community Archives Oral Hostory Collection, Hershey, PA.

Rippon, Rose Reese. March 5, 2007. Interview by Millie Landis-Coyle. Hershey Historical Society, Hershey, PA.

The author also conducted oral interviews with Reese family members: Mary Elizabeth (Reese) Pearson, Robert Hyson Reese, John Manifold Reese, Edward Irons Reese, Ralph Collins Reese, Harry Burnett Reese Jr., Charles Richard (Dick) Reese, Rose Amos (Reese) Rippon, James Rippon, Stanley

Reese, Harry G. (Pat) Lauzon, Brian Lauzon, Shirley Reese, Bobby Reese, Dale Leiphart, Margaret (Peg) (Stuart) Leiphart, Sally Overholt Mason, and Bradley Overholt Reese.

Oral interviews with family friends included: Dick Schell, Jack (Rip) Stover, and Danny Zimmerman.

Publications:

D'Antonio, Michael. *Hershey: Milton S. Hershey's Extraordinary Life of Wealth, Empire, and Utopian Dreams*. New York: Simon & Schuster. 2006.

HERSHEY-REESE & REECO. *Closing Agenda.* Hershey Historical Society, Hershey, PA. June 1, 1963.

REESETTE. A Tribute to George D. McClees. Special Issue. December 29, 1974.

REESETTE. October 1983. Vol. XIV, No. X.

Made in the USA
San Bernardino, CA
09 February 2014